Come In And Worship

Liturgies And Sermons For Holy Week

Robert C. Bankhead

CSS Publishing Company, Inc., Lima, Ohio

COME IN AND WORSHIP

Copyright © 2001 by
CSS Publishing Company, Inc.
Lima, Ohio

The original purchaser may photocopy material in this publication for use as it was intended (i.e., worship material for worship use; educational material for classroom use; dramatic material for staging or production). No additional permission is required from the publisher for such copying by the original purchaser only. Inquiries should be addressed to: Permissions, CSS Publishing Company, Inc., P.O. Box 4503, Lima, Ohio 45802-4503.

For more information about CSS Publishing Company resources, visit our website at www.csspub.com.

ISBN 0-7880-1862-0   PRINTED IN U.S.A.

*In memory
of
Martha Sue Bankhead Boyd*

Table Of Contents

Worship Liturgies

Biblical Liturgies For Holy Week	8
Palm Sunday — *A Festival Procession Of The Palms*	9
Liturgy: Psalm 118:1-2, 19-29	11
Maundy Thursday — *Holy Communion*	16
Liturgy: Mark 14:12-26	18
Good Friday — *Tenebrae*	24
Liturgy: Mark 14:17-72; 15:1-47	27

Proclaiming Good News

Preaching The Gospel Through Holy Week	36
Palm Sunday	37
Sermon: "Open The Gates Of Righteousness"	38
A Time With Children — Sharing The Faith	42
A Children's Story: "The Donkey's Tale"	43
Maundy Thursday	45
Communion Meditation: "Our Paschal Lamb"	46
Good Friday	49
Sermon: "Early In The Morning"	50

Worship Liturgies

Biblical Liturgies For Holy Week

Palm Sunday　　　　　　　　　　Psalm 118:1-2, 19-29
　　"Blessed Is The One Who Comes In The Name Of The Lord"
　　　　A Festival Procession Of The Palms

Maundy Thursday　　　　　　　　　　Mark 14:12-26
　　　"With Friends, In An Upper Room"
　　　　　Holy Communion

Good Friday　　　　　　　　　Mark 14:17-72; 15:1-47
　　　"Tolling The Hours Of The Passion"
　　　Tenebrae — The Service Of Darkness

Biblical Liturgies For Holy Week

Opportunities for lengthy reading of Holy Scripture in worship are limited. The services normally include brief passages read as texts for the Proclamation of the Word, and in some churches, two or more readings from the Lectionary. Believing that the reading of scripture was a central element in the worship of the early church, and that it has continued through the history of the church as a foundation stone for God's people whenever they gather to worship, congregations continually seek occasions to hear the Word of God.

The worship services of Holy Week are marvelous occasions for a congregation to read and hear extended biblical narratives and pericopes. Liturgies that are shaped by the scripture provide an opportunity for the community of faith to join in reading long portions of the Bible on a single occasion for worship.

The Worship for Palm Sunday follows the Royal Psalm 118 as a frame for the liturgy, using the words of the psalmist for prayers and responsive readings. The movement of the Psalm shapes the form of worship and provides its direction.

The liturgies for Maundy Thursday and Good Friday are planned to allow a full reading of the Passion Narrative by using the longer recommended Gospel reading from the Lectionary as a framework for the worship service. Shaping the liturgy around the Gospel Narrative gives an opportunity for the congregation to read and hear the entire biblical account of Jesus' Passion.

Palm Sunday

"Blessed Is The One Who Comes In The Name Of The Lord"

Psalm 118:1-2, 19-29

The Psalter reading for Palm Sunday, Psalm 118:1-2, 19-29, is a royal psalm, a liturgy of coronation for a king, who has returned triumphantly from a victorious campaign. Dressed in full battle armor, wearing a thick leather vest and a helmet on his head, and carrying a heavy shield, with a sharp, broad sword at his side, he came from a fierce battle in which the Israelites had gained a great victory. They had been surrounded by their foes, and it seemed they would be defeated, but they fought valiantly. Miraculously the tide of battle had turned their way, and they won a decisive victory. Tired, dirty, hungry, and thirsty, the king knew that God had given them the victory. Before resting from the battle, he wanted to give thanks. He led the troops up to the gates of the temple. Standing before the huge, massive doors, he cried out to the priests with a loud voice, "Open to me the gates of righteousness, that I may come in and give thanks to the Lord."

The priests threw open the gates and proclaimed to the assembled crowd, "This is the gate of the Lord. Let the righteous come in and worship. Blessed is the one who comes in the name of the Lord." The royal procession marched up to the horns of the altar for the coronation. The crowds joined in the chorus, "Give thanks to the Lord, for God is good. The steadfast love of the Lord endures forever."

The Liturgy for Palm Sunday uses the Psalm as a frame for the adoration of Jesus, King of Kings, who rode triumphantly into Jerusalem on the first day of his last week. Dressed in the simple, common clothes of a peasant, riding on the back of a donkey, tired, hungry, thirsty, Jesus certainly did not look like a king. But the crowds believed him to be the promised ruler who would gather an army and deliver them from the oppression of the hated Romans.

Ripping branches from the bushes of trees along the roadway, and throwing them into his path to form a royal carpet, they sang loudly in praise and adoration, "Blessed is the One who comes in the name of the Lord." They escorted him up to the gates of the Temple, acclaiming him king.

On Palm Sunday the congregation gathers to relive that triumphant procession at the beginning of Holy Week. Again voices sing in adoration, acclaiming him King of Kings and Lord of Lords. Worshipers come to the house of God to give thanks, to sing praise, and to worship our Lord and Savior. The royal Psalm gives a context for the worship and provides a liturgy of praise.

Rubrics
1. For the processional the children might come from their seats with their parents to the front of the sanctuary, carrying palm branches. An alternative to palm branches might be branches from bushes by the side of the road.

2. When the children come to the front, the worship leader may take time for a children's sermon or other occasion for children's worship.

3. The First Lesson might be the scripture text for the morning sermon. The Gospel Lesson should be the Lectionary Reading for Palm Sunday.

4. The Order for the Offering should be adjusted to conform to the customary order of the congregation.

5. The Worship Leader offers the Prayers of the People or Pastoral Prayers.

The Lord's Day

The Worship Of God

Palm Sunday

"Blessed Is The One Who Comes In The Name Of The Lord"

Prelude

An Introit Liturgy

The Call To Worship   Psalm 118:1-2
Leader: Give thanks to the Lord, for God is good.
People: The steadfast love of the Lord endures forever.
Leader: Let all God's people say,
People: The steadfast love of the Lord endures forever.

A Processional Hymn — "Open Now The Gates Of Beauty"

An Invocation   Psalm 118:19-24
Leader: Open to us the gates of righteousness,
People: That we may enter through them and give thanks to the Lord.
Leader: This is the gate of the Lord. The righteous shall enter through it.
People: We thank you, O Lord, that you have answered us and have become our salvation.
Leader: The stone that the builders rejected has become the chief cornerstone.
People: This is the Lord's doing; it is marvelous in our eyes.
Leader: This is the day the Lord has made.
People: Let us rejoice and be glad in it.

A Liturgy Of Penitence

Call To Confession   Psalm 118:25
Leader: Save us, we beseech you, O Lord!
People: O Lord, we beseech you, give us success!

Unison Prayer Of Confession
Mighty and gracious God, whom our Lord, Jesus Christ, called Father, your Son came to the holy city, Jerusalem, humble and meek, riding on a donkey. The crowds prepared a royal way proclaiming him king and singing praise to the one who came in the name of the Lord. We have come to the sanctuary, but we stand idly by, our lips mute, our voices strangely silent. We fail to join in adoration of our King of Kings. We are so busy with our own wishes and desires; we are so consumed by our own passions and lusts; we are so concerned with our own cares and needs, we cannot take time to sing praise. Forgive the selfishness of our lives. Forgive the pettiness of our days. Forgive the pride of our hearts, the arrogance of our minds, the vanity of our souls. Restore to us your salvation through the gift of your Son, and we will sing praise to Jesus Christ, our Lord. Amen.

Silent Prayers Of Confession

The Assurance Of Grace   Psalm 118:26
Leader: Blessed are all who come in the name of the Lord.
People: We bless you from the house of the Lord.
Leader: Blessed are all who believe the gospel, and call upon the name of Jesus Christ for salvation. In Jesus Christ we are redeemed.

The Response — "Gloria Patri"

The Liturgy Of The Word

An Affirmation Of Our Faith　　　　　　　　Psalm 118:27a
Leader: The Lord is God.
People: God has given us light.
Leader: Let us say what we believe.

The Apostles' Creed

A Call To Adore The King　　　　　　　　　Psalm 118:27b
Leader: Bind the festal procession with branches up to the horns of the altar.

Children's Processional Of The Palms

Hymn — "All Glory, Laud, And Honor"

A Time With Children — Sharing The Faith

Prayer For Illumination
God of wisdom and truth, who by priests and prophets called a people and revealed your Word, who by your Son, Incarnate Word of God, has now spoken to all humankind, speak now to us by your holy and inspired Word faithfully written, that we may know your truth, and believe that you are God. Amen.

The Reading Of The Holy Scripture
　　The First Lesson

　　The Gospel Lesson

Proclamation Of The Word

An Ascription Of Praise — or **A Prayer**
With the priests of the temple and the multitudes by the road to Jerusalem, we join to give praise to the Lord our God. We laud and magnify your name, O Holy God. To you at all times and in every place be glory and blessing and thanksgiving, now and forever, world without end. Amen.

A Liturgy Of Response
The Offering Of Tithes And Gifts

The Offertory

Doxology

Prayer Of Dedication

The Morning Prayers   Psalm 118:28-29
Leader: You are my God, and I will give thanks to you.
People: You are my God, I will extol you.
Leader: O give thanks to the Lord, for God is good.
People: The steadfast love of the Lord endures forever.

The Prayers Of Thanks
Leader: Lift up your hearts.
People: We lift them up to the Lord.
Leader: Let us give thanks to the Lord, our God.
People: It is right to give thanks and praise.

Leader: Our prayers of thanks we offer to you, Almighty God, who in the beginning created the heavens and the earth, who made all things and declared them good, who formed us of the dust of the ground and breathed into us the breath of life.
People: Our prayers of thanks we offer to you, Merciful God, who spoke through the ages to holy prophets, who revealed your wisdom and truth, who now has spoken through the Incarnate Word, your Son, Jesus Christ.
Leader: Our prayers of thanks we offer to you, Gracious God, who in your Son came down to earth to dwell among us, who in our Lord, King of Kings, rules over all, who in our Savior, by his death on the cross, has freely forgiven our sins and redeemed us.

People: Our prayers of thanks we offer to you, Loving God, who crowned our lives with glory and honor, providing all we need for abundant life, who gave us love in the intimacy of our families, who taught us fellowship in the community of your people, and gave us peace.

Unison: To you, O God, be glory and honor and majesty and dominion and power and might and thanksgiving.

The Prayers Of The People

The Lord's Prayer

Hymn — "Hosanna, Loud Hosanna"

Charge And Benediction

Leader: Go now into the world, people of God, following Jesus Christ, our Lord. Give praise and faithful witness to the King of Kings. God be with you.

People: And also with you. Amen.

Postlude

Maundy Thursday

"With Friends, In An Upper Room"

Mark 14:12-26

On Maundy Thursday many churches by custom observe the Sacrament of the Lord's Supper. It was on this night Jesus instituted the sacrament and instructed the disciples to repeat it. The service recalls Jesus' last evening meal with the band of twelve, before his arrest, the trials, and his crucifixion. The Synoptic Gospels clearly denote the Last Supper as the Jewish Seder Meal, in observance of Passover, recalling God's providential deliverance of the people of Israel from their bondage in Egypt. The liturgy for the evening may appropriately use prayers and readings from the Seder rite together with the church's ritual for the Lord's Supper.

For Maundy Thursday of Year B in the Lectionary Cycle the account of the Last Supper in the Gospel of Mark 14:12-26 is read. Mark believed the supper was the Passover Meal, and the liturgy includes elements to emphasize the character of a Jewish Seder. The Prayer of Invocation is a *Kiddush* Prayer. The Reading of the Law — *Torah* — recalls Moses' instructions instituting the Seder, Exodus 12:1-27. The traditional four questions of the Seder frame the Reading of the Law. The *Credo* is the Jewish Creed from Deuteronomy 26:5-9. Finally, it is suggested that for the closing hymn one of the Psalms from the *Hallel* — Psalms 113-117 — be sung, as is traditional to close the Seder.

The Liturgy uses Jesus' announcement that one of the twelve will betray him as the Call to Confession of Sin. The Words of Institution of the Lord's Supper are read for the Assurance of Grace. This leads the congregation into observance of the sacrament.

Rubrics
1. It is suggested that the Law — *Torah* — be read by a Reader other than the Liturgist, to highlight this part of the liturgy.

2. The order for celebration of the Eucharist and distribution of the bread and the cup should be adjusted as appropriate for the service in the denomination and for the custom in each worshiping congregation.

3. The Nicene Creed, as the traditional creed for the Sacrament of Holy Communion, is used for the Confession of Faith. The Apostles' Creed may be used as an alternative.

4. The Prayers of the People, or Pastoral Prayer, after the Communion, should be led by the Worship Leader.

The Worship Of God

Maundy Thursday

A Service Of Scripture And Prayer For Holy Communion

"With Friends, In An Upper Room"

Prelude

The Gathering — A Liturgy Of Community

A Call To Worship
The Gospel — Mark 14:12-16

Leader: On the first day of Unleavened Bread, when the Passover Lamb is sacrificed, the disciples said to Jesus,

People: **"Where do you want us to go and make the preparations for you to eat the Passover?"**

Leader: So Jesus sent two of the disciples, saying to them, "Go into the city; and a man carrying a jar of water will meet you. Follow him; and wherever he enters, say to the owner of the house,

People: **'The Teacher asks, "Where is my guest room, where I may eat the Passover with my disciples?"'**

Leader: "He will show you a large room upstairs, furnished and ready. Make preparations for us there."

People: **The disciples set out and went to the city. They found everything as Jesus had told them; and they prepared the Passover Meal.**

A Prayer Of Invocation (*In Unison*)
Kiddush
Blessed art Thou, eternal God, ruler of the universe, creator of the fruit of the vine. Blessed art Thou, who hast chosen us through Thy commandments. Blessed art Thou, who out of Thy love, hast given us this festival of Unleavened Bread. To Thy name be praise. Amen.

A Hymn Of Praise — "The God of Abraham Praise"

The Liturgy Of The Word

The Gospel — Mark 14:17
Leader: When it was evening, Jesus came with the twelve.
People: **What is this night? Why is it different from all other nights?**

The Law — Exodus 12:1-27 — The Torah

Reader: Exodus 12:1-13

Leader: On all other nights we may eat leavened bread.
People: **Why on this night may we eat only unleavened bread?**

Reader: Exodus 12:14-20

Leader: On all other nights we eat all kinds of herbs.
People: **Why on this night do we eat only bitter herbs?**
Leader: On all other nights we need not dip the herbs.
People: **Why on this night do we dip them twice?**
Leader: On all other nights we eat in any manner.
People: **Why on this night do we recline?**

Reader: Exodus 12:21-27

Credo — Deuteronomy 26:5-9

A wandering Aramean was my ancestor; he went down into Egypt and lived there as an alien, few in number, and there he became a nation, mighty and populous. When the Egyptians treated us harshly and afflicted us, by imposing hard labor on us, we cried to the Lord, the God of our ancestors. The Lord heard our voice and saw our affliction, our toil, and our oppression. The Lord brought us up out of Egypt with a mighty hand and an outstretched arm, with a terrifying display of power and with signs and wonders. And he brought us into this place, and gave us this land, a land flowing with milk and honey.

The Reading Of Scripture — Text for Preaching the Word

Meditation

An Inscription Of Praise — or **A Prayer**

The Liturgy Of The Table

A Call To Confession
The Gospel — Mark 14:18-21

Leader: When they had taken their places and were eating, Jesus said, "Truly I tell you, one of you will betray me; one who is eating with me."

People: **They began to be distressed, and to say to him, one after another, "Surely not I?"**

Leader: He said to them, "It is one of the twelve; one who is dipping bread into the bowl with me. For the Son of Man goes as it is written of him. But woe to that one by whom the Son of Man is betrayed.

People: **It would have been better for that one not to have been born."**

Unison Prayer Of Confession

Surely, not I, Lord! Even if I were offered riches, or prestige, or power, I would not betray you. Even if my life were in danger, I would not deny you. Lord, is it I? Who have betrayed your trust? Who have run in fear when I should have been loyal? Who have deserted my friends? Ignored my neighbors? Gracious God, you are aware of my sin. Cleanse me by your forgiveness. Wash away the stain of my sinfulness. Make my heart pure within me. Protect and preserve me from all evil, and deliver me from the power of sin, that redeemed and restored, I may be a loyal disciple of my Lord, Jesus Christ. Amen.

Silent Prayers of Confession

An Assurance Of Grace
The Gospel — Mark 14:22-24

Leader: While they were eating, Jesus took a loaf of bread, and after blessing it, he broke it and gave it to them, and said, "Take; this is my body."

People: **Then he took a cup, and after giving thanks, he gave it to them, and all of them drank from it. He said to them, "This is my blood of the covenant, which is poured out for many."**

Leader: Believe the good news of the gospel, my friends. By the body of Christ, we are saved; by the blood of Christ, we are redeemed; by the love of Christ, we are saved.

The Invitation To The Lord's Table

Hymn — "O Sacred Head Now Wounded"

The Confession Of Faith — The Nicene Creed

The Great Prayer Of Thanksgiving
Leader: The Lord be with you.
People: And also with you.
Leader: Lift up your hearts.
People: We lift them up to the Lord.
Leader: Let us give thanks to the Lord, our God.
People: It is right to give thanks and praise.
Leader: O Holy God! Almighty creator of heaven and earth. You made us and breathed into us the breath of life. You gave us bread to eat and the fruit of the vine to drink. With joy we give you thanks and praise.
People: O Holy God! Merciful Father of our Lord, Jesus Christ. You sent your beloved Son a servant to wash away our sinful pride and feed us with the bread of life. With joy we give you thanks for this feast with him who died for us.
Leader: O Holy God! Ever present Holy Spirit. To prophets you spoke with words of truth and you speak to us still. You have come to dwell among us and in us and with us. With joy we give you thanks for your presence.
People: Holy! Holy! Holy! Lord God of Hosts. Blessed Trinity! Creator, Redeemer, and Giver of Life. We sing your praise.
Leader: We give thanks that on the night before he died our Lord Jesus took bread, gave thanks, broke it and gave it to the disciples, saying, "Take, eat. This is my body."
People: We give you thanks that in like manner Jesus took the cup, saying, "This is the new covenant in my blood poured out for many."
Leader: We give you thanks that he commanded us, "Do this in remembrance of me."
People: In remembrance of your mighty acts in Jesus Christ, we take this bread and drink this cup, and give you praise and thanksgiving. Amen.

The Communion Of The Bread And The Cup

The Prayers Of The People

The Lord's Prayer

The Sending — A Liturgy Of Benediction

The Gospel — Mark 14:25-26
Leader: Jesus said, "Truly, I tell you, I will never again drink of the fruit of the vine, until that day when I drink it new in the Kingdom of God."
People: When they had sung the hymn, they went out to the Mount of Olives.

Hymn   **Hallel**
"Sing Praise Unto The Name Of God" — Psalm 113

The Dismissal
Leader: Go now into the night, O people of God, strengthened in faith by God's presence, nourished in spirit by Christ's body and blood, inspired in hope by God's Spirit. May God be with you.
People: And with all God's people. Amen.

Postlude

Good Friday

"Tolling The Hours Of The Passion"

Mark 14:17-72; 15:1-47

Tenebrae — The Service of Darkness is an ancient form of worship, dating from the fourth century. Traditionally the service evolves as candles are extinguished and the sanctuary is gradually darkened to remind worshipers of the darkness that covered the earth at the death of Jesus Christ. It culminates in the darkness at noon as Jesus hung on the cross.

The service is highly dramatic. It begins in quiet reverence with the lighting of the candles and prayer, then proceeds as the candles are extinguished one by one with scripture readings and prayers, symbolizing the descent of the world into darkness. As the service draws to a close, the sanctuary is almost totally dark, recalling the despair of the disciples at the death of Jesus and their hopelessness on Holy Saturday as the body of Jesus lay in the tomb. The mood is one of shock, gloom, grief, and sadness as the congregation relives the depth of Christ's suffering and death.

Helping the worshipers realize the total impact of the darkest day for believers in Jesus Christ, Tenebrae prepares for the glorious renewal of life in Christ's resurrection on Easter. The startling contrast of the darkness of Good Friday with the dawning new light of Easter Sunday heightens the joyous celebration of light. One candle, symbolizing Jesus as the Light of the World, burns throughout the service of darkness and remains burning at the close of the worship, one single light that is never extinguished. The light came into the world and the darkness cannot overcome it. On Easter Sunday, with the dawning of the day, the light bursts forth from the depth of the empty tomb in the full and glorious Light of Life. Jesus Christ has risen, and is alive forevermore.

The liturgy for Year B of the Lectionary Cycle is shaped by reading the Passion Narrative from the Gospel of Mark. It allows the entire narrative to be read as the order of worship develops.

Mark's account of the death of Jesus is shaped by the notes of time on the day of crucifixion. The liturgy for Tenebrae is formed by the numbering of the hours, recalling the death of Jesus Christ.

Rubrics
1. Eight candles should be prepared. They might be arranged in a circle as a clock to call attention to the hours of the cross, which is featured in Mark's account of the crucifixion. The candles should be lit at the beginning of the service with a prayer for Lighting the Festival Lights from the Seder.

2. Seven of the candles will be extinguished during the service, as symbol of the descending darkness. The eighth candle should remain burning at the close of the service. It represents the continuing light of Jesus Christ, the Light of the World.

3. It is suggested that at the moment of the sixth hour of the Passion, the lights of the sanctuary be extinguished to signify the darkness of the cross at noon. At this point the sanctuary will be completely dark except for the remaining candles and the light for the reader to read the Gospel.

4. The Scripture Readings include both responsive readings by the congregation and passages that are read by a Reader other than the worship leader.

5. At the close of the service it is suggested that the Liturgist close the open Pulpit Bible, which will remain closed until Easter Sunday morning. It symbolizes the day the body of Jesus, the Incarnate Word, lay in the tomb. The Bible may be carried from the sanctuary or left closed on the pulpit.

6. The Bible then is opened at the beginning of the first service of Easter to signify the return of the Word of God to the sanctuary. If the Bible was carried from the sanctuary, an elder or other member of the congregation might carry it back into the

sanctuary, place it on the pulpit, and open it to begin the first worship of Easter Sunday.

7. The service concludes in silence as the worshipers leave the sanctuary. There is no postlude.

The Worship Of God

Good Friday

Tenebrae — The Service Of Darkness

"Tolling The Hours Of The Passion"

Prelude

The Gathering — A Liturgy Of Community

6:00 p.m. Passover Begins

Lighting The Candles
Leader: Blessed art Thou, O Lord, Our God, King of all creation. You sanctified us by your commandments, and commanded us to light the Festival Lights.
People: **You kept us alive, and sustained us, and brought us to this season. May our community of faith be consecrated by the light of your love, and may it shine upon us, and bring us peace.**

The Gospel — Mark 14:17-19
Leader: When it was evening, Jesus came with the twelve.
People: **When they had taken their places, and were eating, Jesus said, "Truly I tell you, one of you will betray me, one who is eating with me."**
Leader: They began to be distressed, and to say to him, one after another,
People: **"Surely, not I?"**

Prayer Of Invocation (*In Unison*)
Gracious God, dare we call this day good, when it recalls the Passion of your Son, our Lord? Dare we worship you on this night, when we remember the suffering and death of Jesus Christ? Dare we sing praise in the community of friends, when it reminds us of the betrayal, and denial, and desertion of his friends? Come to us in the depth of your love these moments of quiet remembrance. Speak to us of sorrow and of joy, of denial and of triumph, that we may find in the crucifixion your gift of reconciliation and peace. Keep us in communion with you, and in community with one another, that we may worship in spirit and in truth. Amen.

The Gospel — Mark 14:22-24

Leader: While they were eating, Jesus took a loaf of bread, and after blessing it, he broke it, and gave it to them and said, "Take; this is my body."

People: **Then he took a cup, and after giving thanks, he gave it to them, and all of them drank from it. He said to them, "This is my blood of the covenant, which is poured out for many."**

Hymn — "Were You There When They Crucified My Lord?" or "Beneath The Cross Of Jesus"

A Liturgy Of Penitence

9:00 p.m. — In The Garden

The Gospel — Mark 14:26-31

Leader: When they had sung the hymn, they went out to the Mount of Olives. And Jesus said to them, "You will all become deserters, for it is written, 'I will strike the shepherd, and the sheep will be scattered.' But after I am raised up, I will go before you to Galilee."

People: **Peter said to Jesus, "Even though all become deserters, I will not."**

Leader: Jesus said to Peter, "Truly I tell you, this day, this very night, before the cock crows twice, you will deny me three times."

People: But Peter said vehemently, "Even though I must die with you, I will not deny you." And all of them said the same.

Prayers Of Confession (*In Unison*)

Gracious God, you know our frailty; you understand our weakness; you are acquainted with our failures. Though we have professed to believe, we betray our Lord by our actions. Though we have promised to follow, we deny our Christ by our selfishness. Though we have vowed to be faithful, we desert our Savior by our own desires. We have lived for ourselves and abandoned our neighbors. We have refused to bear the troubles of others. We have ignored the pain of the world, and passed by the hungry, the poor, and the oppressed. In your great mercy, forgive our sins, and free us from all evil, that we may choose your will, and obey your commandments, through Jesus Christ, our Savior. Amen.

Assurance Of Pardon

The Liturgy Of The Word

Meditation — Proclamation Of The Word

An Ascription Of Praise — or A Prayer

The Service Of Darkness

I. The Gospel — Mark 14:32-42
A Reader

Hymn — "Go To Dark Gethsemane,"
  or " 'Tis Midnight, And On Olive's Brow"

12:00 Midnight — Betrayal and Arrest

II. The Gospel — Mark 14:43-52

Leader: Immediately, while he was speaking, Judas, one of the twelve, arrived. With him there was a crowd, with swords and clubs, from the chief priests, the scribes, and the elders.

People: **Now the betrayer had given them a sign, saying, "The one I will kiss is the man; arrest him and lead him away under guard."**

Leader: So when he came he went up to Jesus at once and said, "Rabbi!" And kissed him. Then they laid hands on Jesus and arrested him.

People: **But one of those who stood near drew his sword, and struck the slave of the high priest, cutting off his ear.**

Leader: Then Jesus said to them, "Have you come out with swords and clubs to arrest me as though I were a bandit? Day after day I was with you in the temple teaching, and you did not arrest me. But let the scriptures be fulfilled."

People: **All of them deserted him and fled. A certain young man was following him, wearing nothing but a linen cloth. They caught hold of him, but he left the linen cloth, and ran off naked.**

The First Candle Is Extinguished
It is the Candle recalling Judas' betrayal and Jesus' arrest.

3:00 a.m. — The Sanhedrin Trial

III. The Gospel — Mark 14:53-65
A Reader

The Second Candle Is Extinguished
It is the Candle recalling Jesus' mock trial before the Jewish court.

IV. The Gospel — Mark 14:66-72

Leader: While Peter was below in the courtyard, one of the servant girls of the high priest came by. When she saw Peter warming himself, she stared at him, and said, "You also were with Jesus, the man from Nazareth."

People: But he denied it, saying, "I do not know or understand what you are talking about." And he went out into the forecourt. Then the cock crowed.

Leader: And the servant girl, on seeing him, began again to say to the bystanders, "This man is one of them."

People: But again he denied it.

Leader: Then after a little while the bystanders again said to Peter, "Certainly you are one of them; for you are a Galilean."

People: But he began to curse, and he swore an oath. "I do not know this man you are talking about." At that moment the cock crowed for the second time.

Leader: Then Peter remembered that Jesus had said to him, "Before the cock crows twice, you will deny me three times."

People: And he broke down and wept.

The Third Candle Is Extinguished
It is the Candle recalling Peter's denial.

6:00 a.m. — The Roman Trial

V. The Gospel — Mark 15:1-15

Leader: As soon as it was morning, the chief priests held a consultation with the elders and scribes and the whole council. They bound Jesus, led him away, and handed him over to Pilate.

People: Pilate asked him, "Are you the King of the Jews?"

Leader: Jesus answered him, "You say so." Then the chief priests accused him of many things.

People: Pilate asked him again, "Have you no answer? See how many charges they bring against you."

Leader: But Jesus made no further reply, so that Pilate was amazed.

People: Now at the festival he used to release a prisoner for them, anyone for whom they asked.

Leader: Now a man called Barabbas was in prison with the rebels who had committed murder during the insurrection. So the crowd came and began to ask Pilate to do for them according to his custom.

People: Then Pilate answered them, "Do you want me to release for you the King of the Jews?" For he realized that it was out of jealousy that the chief priests had handed him over.

Leader: But the chief priests stirred up the crowd to have him release Barabbas for them instead.

People: Pilate spoke to them again, "Then what do you wish me to do with the man you call the King of the Jews?"

Leader: They shouted back, "Crucify him!"

People: Pilate asked them, "Why? What evil has he done?"

Leader: But they shouted all the more, "Crucify him!"

People: So Pilate, wishing to satisfy the crowd, released Barabbas for them; and after flogging Jesus, he handed him over to be crucified.

The Fourth Candle Is Extinguished
　　It is the Candle recalling Jesus' trial by Pontius Pilate and the release of Barabbas.

VI. The Gospel — Mark 15:16-20
A Reader

The Fifth Candle Is Extinguished
　　It is the Candle recalling the mockery and derision of Jesus by the soldiers.

9:00 a.m. — The Crucifixion

VII. The Gospel — Mark 15:21-32
A Reader

The Sixth Candle Is Extinguished
It is the Candle recalling Jesus' crucifixion.

12:00 Noon — Darkness

VIII. The Gospel — Mark 15:33
Leader: When it was noon, darkness came over the whole land until three in the afternoon.

The Sanctuary Lights Are Extinguished

A Minute Of Silence

3:00 p.m. — Death

IX. The Gospel — Mark 15:34-41
A Reader

The Seventh Candle Is Extinguished
It is the Candle recalling the death of Jesus, the Son of God.

One Candle Remains — The Candle Of The Light Of The World
It is the Candle that can never be extinguished, for the Light came into the world and brought life to all humankind. The Light shines in the darkness, and the darkness cannot overcome it.

The Lights Of The Sanctuary Are Relit

Evening Prayers — Prayers Of The People

X. The Gospel — Mark 15:42-47

Leader: When evening had come, and since it was the day of preparation, that is, the day before the Sabbath, Joseph of Arimathea, a respected member of the council, who was also himself waiting expectantly for the Kingdom of God, went boldly to Pilate, and asked for the body of Jesus.

People: Then Pilate wondered if Jesus were already dead; and summoning the centurion, he asked him whether Jesus had been dead for some time. When he learned from the centurion that Jesus was dead, he granted the body to Joseph.

Leader: Then Joseph bought a linen cloth, and taking down the body, wrapped it in the linen cloth, and laid it in a tomb that had been hewn out of the rock. He then rolled a stone against the door of the tomb.

People: Mary Magdalene and Mary the mother of Joses saw where the body was laid.

Closing The Pulpit Bible

6:00 p.m. — Sabbath Begins

The Dismissal

Leader: Go now into the darkening night, O people of God. Though we walk in darkness, we are not forsaken. We are led by the hand of God. May the love of God calm your fears; may the grace of God keep you through the night; may the presence of God sustain you through life. God be with you.

People: And with all God's people. Amen.

Proclaiming Good News

Preaching The Gospel Through Holy Week

Palm Sunday
      Sermon: "Open The Gates Of Righteousness"
      Texts: Psalm 118:19-29 and Mark 1:1-11

A Time With Children — Sharing The Faith
      Story: "The Donkey's Tale"

Maundy Thursday
      Communion Meditation: "Our Paschal Lamb"
      Texts: 1 Corinthians 5:6-8 and Mark 14:1-2, 12-16

Good Friday
      Sermon: "Early In The Morning"
      Text: Mark 15:1-32

Preaching The Gospel Through Holy Week

Holy Week presents the greatest challenge of the Christian Year to the preacher. The Gospel Narrative takes its readers from the height of joyous celebration at Jesus' Triumphal Entry into Jerusalem, through the meditative spiritual experience of the Last Supper, and the agonizing prayer in the Garden of Gethsemane, to the depth of grief at the crucifixion on Mount Calvary. Each episode prepares believers for the ecstatic joy of Jesus' resurrection. Holy Week is an emotional journey of joy and sorrow, of ecstasy and despair, of celebration and grief. The preacher of the gospel is called to lead the congregation through the full spectrum of emotion, and to do it with a dignity and integrity that does not belittle or trivialize the depth of the gospel.

Retelling the story with creative imagination, the preacher leads the hearers to see the picture with a new perspective, encouraging them to engage both mind and heart in reliving the gospel. The preacher should embrace the full drama of the narrative, both its comedy and its tragedy, for there is both laughter and grief as Jesus walks the road to the cross. Holy Week takes the worshipers from the scene of Jesus riding a small donkey into Jerusalem, through the trail of tears to the crucifixion. It reveals a humble king to whom the multitudes sang praise in a coronation procession. The worshipers see Jesus sad and discouraged as he predicted Judas' betrayal, Peter's denial, and the desertion of all the disciples. They share with Jesus the moving spiritual discipline of reenacting the Exodus from Egypt and the observance of Passover. They watch his agony praying for God to deliver him from the Passion. The worshipers are bystanders at the frightening moment of arrest, observers through the tedious trials, and witnesses to the inescapable sentence of death. They laugh at the ludicrous antics of the high priest tearing his robes or the childish gesture of Pilate trying to wash the guilt of innocent blood from his hands. They weep with the women watching Jesus nailed to the cross and dying. Through each scene the preacher steers the worshiping community of faith through the narrow road between sentimental, unbridled emotion and cold, rationalized logic, to help the hearers walk the road to the cross with Jesus.

Palm Sunday

The challenge of preaching on Palm Sunday is to celebrate the Triumphal Entry of Jesus into Jerusalem without losing sight of his impending Passion. The crowds, who were ready to crown him King, would demand his death before the week was over. The theme for the day reflects the dilemma of the Lectionary calendar, which forces us to choose between observing this Sunday at the beginning of Holy Week as either Passion Sunday or Palm Sunday. A dynamic tension to the day must be recognized if the broad context of the Passion Narrative is observed. It is never satisfactory simply to acclaim Jesus King, unless it is remembered he was a humble monarch who would never be the military leader the crowds expected him to be, and would be crucified.

In the life of the Christian church, Palm Sunday seems out of place. The season of Lent with its spiritual exercises of prayer and self-denial draws to a close, suddenly we find ourselves in a day of celebration, a festival of rejoicing and gaiety. Then, with an abrupt shock we are thrown from the height of rejoicing to the depth of despair, rushing to Maundy Thursday and Good Friday, with their remembrance of the crucifixion and death of Jesus at Calvary. We are on a roller coaster of religious emotion, with little time to adjust to the abrupt change Palm Sunday brings.

The story of Palm Sunday is incongruous. It is a comical farce to see a man, dressed in common, dirty clothes, riding along a dusty road on the back of a young donkey, while multitudes of people are shouting praise, running frantically alongside to pay him honor, proclaiming him King. It is also a tragic drama, for even as we hear them singing, "Hosanna in the highest! Blessed is the One who comes in the name of the Lord!" we know that but a few short days later these same multitudes will gather before the palace to shout, "Crucify Him! CRUCIFY HIM!" and demand his death.

The celebration of Palm Sunday honestly addresses both the jubilation and the despair as the congregation worships the King who refused to be the ruler for whom the crowds were looking. The preacher of the gospel leads the worshipers along the road both to sing praise and to weep, to rejoice and to mourn.

Open The Gates Of Righteousness

Texts: Psalm 118:19-29 and Mark 1:1-11

Knock! Knock! Knock!

The king stood before the huge, massive gates of the temple. Dressed in battle armor, wearing a thick, leather vest, a helmet on his head; he carried a heavy shield and a sharp, broad sword at his side.

He had returned from a fierce battle. The Israelites had been victorious over their enemies. It had been hard fought and dangerous. They had been surrounded by their foes, and it seemed they would be defeated, when suddenly the momentum of battle had turned their way, and they had gained a great victory.

Tired, hungry, and dirty, the king first led the troops to the temple. He knew that it was the hand of God who had given them victory, and he wanted to give thanks.

He knocked on the heavy wooden door, shouting, "Open to me the Gates of Righteousness, that I may come in, and give thanks to the Lord!"

The priests threw open the doors and announced to the assembled crowd, "This is the Gate of the Lord! Let the righteous come in and worship."

The king led the way into the temple to offer praise and thanksgiving. And the crowd responded with choruses of praise, adoration, and faith. "Blessed is the One who comes in the name of the Lord!"

Another king! Another time! Another triumphal entry! Jesus came into the city of Jerusalem, dressed in the simple clothes of a peasant, common, ordinary, and unpretentious, riding on the back of a donkey.

The little beast plodded along the dusty road. The disciples had covered its back with their cloaks to provide a makeshift saddle, upon which Jesus sat. His legs were too long; his feet dragged on the ground.

The crowd recognized him, and sang loudly in praise, adoration, and faith. "Hosanna! Blessed is the One who comes in the name of the Lord!" What the priests of the temple cried out in Psalm 118, the multitudes of Jerusalem echoed that first Palm Sunday.

Yet another time! Yet another triumphal entry! Again the king is Jesus the Lord! On Palm Sunday we enter the sanctuary of the house of God, following our king. We come to this holy place to give thanks, to praise, and to adore. We pass through the gates of righteousness to worship.

We celebrate this festive occasion, remembering Jesus' Triumphal Entry. Led by children, waving Palm Branches, we come, rejoicing, and singing, "Hosanna in the highest! Blessed is the One who comes in the name of the Lord!" We join the priests of the temple and the multitudes of Jerusalem to praise the Lord. Yet our worship this day is tempered with our remembrance of Christ's sacrifice by which we are saved.

Palm Sunday ends the season of Lent. Lent is a time of penitence and confession, a time to review our lives. Reverently we consider who we are and what we have been. We remember our struggle with sin, our wrestling with temptation. Lent allows us to acknowledge and confess that we are sinners. With no hope except in the grace and mercy of God, we fervently pray for forgiveness.

Like the king who had been surrounded by his enemies, fearful for his life, facing certain death, we call upon the Lord for deliverance. Palm Sunday then brings us to the doors of the house of God to worship. We rejoice in the mercy of God, and give thanks for God's salvation.

What are these doors of the sanctuary through which we pass to worship?

1. The Psalmist named them gates of righteousness; the priests called them the gates of the Lord. We call them gates of salvation. They are gates of deliverance, gates of freedom from our struggle.

Sometimes we feel that everything is closing in around us, like the king in battle, as if we are surrounded with more than we can handle and there is no escape. There are too many decisions to make, too many things to think about at one time.

- How can we help our children through the drug culture?
- What can we do about our marriage that seems to be going downhill?

- What shall we do about our aging parents?
- How are we going to pay the bills?
- What should we do about our job that has become a burden?
- How can we fill up the long hours of retirement?
- Can we really be free from the temptations that keep sneaking up on us?

We sometimes wish we could just get away from it all, that we could just put everything down for a little while, and escape. We think we will go to the sanctuary, to get away from the troubles of the world.

The house of God is our sanctuary, but not to escape the troubles of the world. It is our holy place to discover and celebrate God's righteousness. In this place God protects us. The powers of evil that surround us in the world dare not enter here. The temptations that challenge us have no power here. Those with whom we compete in the workplace, to get ahead; those who criticize and undermine us and try to tear us down; those who attack us and accuse us in our suspicious, hostile society cannot pursue us here. These are the gates of righteousness. This is the house of God. This is the sanctuary of a loving community of faith.

In this place God sets us free from our burdens. The pain with which we live each day; the anxiety and worry that is ever near; the doubt, uncertainty, and fear cannot reach us here. Here we are surrounded by the promises and assurances of God. The broken relationships, the bickering and quarrels, with our husband, our wife, our teenagers, our parents, with our friends, our colleagues; the worry over ill and aging parents can be put in a new perspective here. Here we know that God is with us, and that we are among God's people. In this place our cares are covered by the righteousness of God.

2. These are the gates of thanksgiving. We enter this place rejoicing and singing. The temple priests invite us to rejoice and be glad in the day the Lord has made. The Psalmist urges us to give thanks to the Lord, for God is good.

Too often the doors of the sanctuary are frightening. We enter hesitantly, with apprehension. We think of the sanctuary as a place of reverence and quiet dignity. We tell our children to be quiet, threatening them with bodily punishment if they dare make any noise. "Just wait till I get you home!" we growl.

Is it any wonder they are afraid to come to church, afraid to come to the sanctuary? They would rather stay in the nursery, where it is all right to talk aloud. We are hesitant to sing very loudly, afraid someone will hear us.

Perhaps we are afraid God will hear us. And so we whisper our songs of praise.

"Hosanna! Loud Hosanna!" Not too loudly!

"All Glory, Laud and Honor, To Thee Redeemer Praise!" Quiet now!

"Allelujah!" Hush!

If anyone were to shout, "Hosanna!" we would rise up from these pews in shocked dismay. How dare anyone disturb the reverence of this place! Reverence does not require the somber, solemn tones of a funeral parlor. Dignity does not need to be repressed and subdued.

Can you imagine in the temple? Can you imagine the king knocking on the doors demanding to be allowed to come in, and the priests sternly exhorting him, "Hush! Even if you did win the battle, don't disturb us."

Can you imagine on the road to Jerusalem? Can you imagine the crowds announcing, "Jesus is coming!" and the multitudes replying quietly, "That's nice, just don't make too much noise."

We can rejoice in the sanctuary. We can sing. For the sanctuary is a place of joy. These are gates of thanksgiving. Reverence can be served with laughter and song. Dignity can be honored with sparkling eyes and a joyful, hearty smile.

In this place we give thanks to God, for we have come to rejoice and be glad. We acknowledge our faith in God. We find in this place the presence of a loving God who is our constant shield and strength.

Open now the gates of the Lord! Enter the gates of righteousness! And worship! Sing and rejoice! This is the house of the Lord! This is the day the Lord has made! Let us rejoice and be glad in it.

Enter these gates with thanksgiving, and praise the name of the Lord!

A Time With Children — Sharing The Faith

Palm Sunday is a natural occasion for time with children in the worship service. A processional of palm branches is an opportunity to meet with children and youth at the front of the sanctuary to share the gospel story with them. As they come waving their palm branches, the congregation sings a hymn, such as "Hosanna, Loud Hosanna," or "All Glory, Laud and Honor." When they reach the front, the preacher might sit on the floor with them and tell a story, such as "The Donkey's Tale."

For visual reinforcement, a member of the congregation dressed in the battle armor of ancient times might be present. There might be a picture of Jesus riding the donkey to show the children. Young children might be given a picture of the Triumphal Entry and crayons. Older children might distribute palm branches to the congregation.

The Donkey's Tale

I'm just a lowly donkey. People make fun of me, kidding me that I'm stubborn. But once upon a time I did something very important. I carried a king into the city of Jerusalem. He rode on my back all the way from Jericho to the big temple in the Holy City. There were crowds of people along the way, shouting and singing, and following along the road. They tore off branches from the trees and bushes and threw them on the road for me to walk on. It was a wonderful day, like a big parade. Everyone was encouraging me. No one was laughing at me then.

The day started strangely. About the middle of the morning, I was tied to a fence post in the master's yard, nibbling on some hay, when two strangers walked up to me. They had full beards, and their clothes were dirty, like they had walked a long way on dusty roads. One of them looked at me, then nodded to his friend, and said, "I think this is the one Jesus sent us to find." The other agreed and said, "Let's take it." I didn't have any idea what they meant. They began to untie me, without even asking my master for permission. I was shocked. Some of the neighbors standing around were also shocked. They tried to stop them, shouting, "Hey! What are you doing? Why are you untying the donkey?" The two men explained that the Lord needed me. I didn't understand, but my master seemed to know what it meant, and he let the two men lead me back to Jericho.

When we got there, they took me to a young man who had the kindest face I had ever seen. His smile seemed to stretch from ear to ear and his eyes were bright. He came over to me and scratched my ear and patted my neck and talked to me. He was so gentle I felt wonderful, and I liked him immediately. He told me his name was Jesus and we were going to do something together.

Some other men took their cloaks off and laid them on me. Jesus climbed on my back. I had never had anyone sit on me before, and I didn't know what to do. He reached up and patted my shoulder and said, "It's going to be okay." He wasn't heavy and I could carry him easily. The two men who had brought me took my rope and led me out onto the road. As we walked, the crowds alongside the road got bigger and bigger, and they began to shout and sing. They kept calling Jesus a king. He didn't look much like a king to me. He seemed to be just a simple man. His robe was ordinary, and he didn't have a crown. I thought if he were a king, he was certainly not like any king people around here usually expect.

When we stopped to rest, I looked at him. He still was smiling in a gentle way, but his eyes weren't sparkling. They were kind of sad and thoughtful, as if he knew something the crowd didn't know. He seemed to realize they didn't really understand what they were doing. I felt like he knew he would never be a king like they wanted. He was too kind and gentle. He knew they would turn against him.

When we got to Jerusalem they led me to the gates of the big temple. Jesus got off my back and gave me a big pat on the head and thanked me for carrying him to Jerusalem. He called me a good colt, and I was very happy. Then he walked up the steps into the temple, and I wondered if I would ever see him again. The two men who had come to get me led me back home and tied me up and thanked my owner for letting me carry Jesus.

I did see Jesus again. It was about five days later. My owner had ridden me to Jerusalem for a big festival, and we spent the night. Early the next morning I was nibbling grass by the city gate when a crowd of people came through the gate. In the middle was Jesus surrounded by a bunch of soldiers. His face was bruised and puffy, and there was dried blood on it. He was wearing a crown, but it was made from a thorn bush. His hands were tied and he had shackles on his feet, and he stumbled along the path. He was carrying a cross, and when he fell down, the soldiers grabbed another man out of the crowd and made him help Jesus carry the cross. The crowds were shouting again, but this time they were cursing him and laughing at him. I wanted to go over and offer to carry Jesus again, but I was tied up and couldn't get through the crowd. He saw me, and he smiled as if he wanted to say, "Now you can see what I knew was going to happen."

The crowd moved on down the road and disappeared. I heard some people talking. They said the soldiers were taking Jesus out to Mount Calvary to kill him. I was very sad. He wasn't the kind of king the people wanted.

Maundy Thursday

The Sacrament of the Lord's Supper is traditional on the evening of Maundy Thursday. It recalls the night Jesus instituted the sacrament with a solemn command for the disciples to repeat it. In the Synoptic Gospels the gathering of the disciples for Jesus' last supper with them was the Jewish Seder Meal, in observance of Passover, reenacting God's providential deliverance of the Israelites from their bondage in Egypt. Traditional themes for preaching the gospel on Maundy Thursday include among others:
- the Passion of Jesus, remembering his death as the Paschal Lamb of God, slain for the sins of the world;
- Institution of the Lord's Supper, with the drama of Judas' betrayal and Peter's denial;
- God's New Covenant with a new chosen people;
- the Unity of the Church symbolized by one bread, one cup; and
- the fervent prayer of Jesus in the Garden of Gethsemane, preparing himself for the ordeal he must face, and pleading God's will be done.

The tone and demeanor of the proclamation might be appropriately earnest prayer and quiet meditation. It is a time for remembrance of the Lord's death, an occasion for reflection on the means of grace, a moment to recall the mighty acts of God to deliver and save a chosen people.

Even though it recalls Jesus' impending death, it is not an evening of unrelieved grief and sorrow. It leads us to prepare ourselves for reliving the crucifixion of Jesus Christ for our salvation, and the ecstasy of the glorious resurrection. The preaching reflects the sure and certain faith that by the death of Jesus we are saved, by his resurrection from the grave we are born again to everlasting life.

Our Paschal Lamb

Texts: 1 Corinthians 5:6-8; Mark 14:1-2, 12-16

O Lamb of God, that takest away the sins of the world;
Have mercy upon us.

It was for the Jewish Passover that Jesus met with the disciples in the Upper Room for his Last Supper with them. Mark makes very clear that the meal was the Jewish Seder, their annual observance of God's deliverance of the Israelite slaves from their bondage in Egypt. Mark calls attention to the fact that it was the first day of Unleavened Bread, when the Paschal Lambs were sacrificed.

For the Israelites, Passover was the most significant, most important event in their history. It was their moment of birth, as a people, and as a nation. Followed by the Exodus from Egypt and their deliverance from oppression, Passover brought them into being and established them as God's chosen people.

It is no wonder they looked back to the night of anxious, frightened waiting, when the angel of the Lord passed over their houses, the very houses which they had marked with the blood of an innocent lamb. The blood of the lamb protected all in the house from the power of death. It is no wonder that Moses, acting as God instructed him, commanded the Israelites to observe the Passover every year in remembrance of God's deliverance. It is no wonder they instructed their children diligently in the meaning of this holy act of commemoration, by which they became God's holy people. It was Passover that defined their nature and character. They were a chosen, freed, and protected people of God.

O Lamb of God, that takest away the sins of the world;
Have mercy upon us.

In the evening Jesus gathered the band of friends who had followed him through his three years of earthly ministry, this community of faithful disciples whom he had called and trained to be the nucleus of a new people of God, the new Israel. Jesus fully understood the significance of the Paschal Lamb, and knew it was He who was the Lamb of God. As they were eating he took the single loaf of bread, broke it into pieces, and passed it to the disciples with the solemn declaration, "This is my body, which is broken for you." When they had eaten, Jesus poured out wine into a goblet, and passed it to them, again with the solemn declaration, "This is my blood of the new covenant poured out for the forgiveness of sins." With these word Jesus instituted the Sacrament of the Lord's Supper. Observing this sacrament, eating this bread, and drinking this cup, we are united with Christ, our Paschal Lamb, by whose blood we are redeemed. We are united in the community of faith with all who by the grace of God are saved.

O Lamb of God, that takest away the sins of the world;
Grant us your peace.

Paul, writing to the Christians in Corinth, claimed that Christ, our Paschal Lamb, has been sacrificed for us. The death of Christ theologically fulfilled the slaying of the Paschal Lamb. Christ is the Lamb sacrificed to shield, to protect, and to deliver us from that death which was the punishment of a just and righteous God against those who refused to obey the will of God.

When we gather to observe the sacrament of Holy Communion in remembrance of Jesus' Last Supper with the disciples, we renew our faith in Jesus as the Paschal Lamb slain for our redemption. We eat the broken bread of his body; we sip the poured wine, acknowledging our sinfulness, and affirm our faith in the grace of God to save us.

The sacrifice of the Lamb of God is our moment of birth, as a people of God. It is the holy act of God who chose us and loves us, to set us free from the bondage, to deliver us from the slavery of sin. It is the most significant event by which we become who we are, God's own people. Followed by the resurrection of Christ from the dead, his sacrificial death defines our nature and character. It makes us who we are.

We are God's chosen people, set free from the bondage of sin. We are delivered from the evil and wickedness of our rebellious nature. We are God's beloved sinners, forgiven by the sacrifice of Christ, the Lamb of God.

Paul's identification of Christ as our Paschal Lamb occurs in the context of his moral instructions. He was exhorting the Corinthians not to tolerate the gross immorality that was present even in the church. Paul was determined to bring them to their senses and remind them of the moral character that is required of the community of those who believe in Christ.

Paul used the metaphor of leaven, which was very familiar to the Jews, to encourage the Christians in Corinth to remove all the evil and wickedness that was present in their lives. As the Jews removed all leaven from their homes in preparation for the observance of Passover, Paul exhorted the Corinthians to purge themselves of gross immorality. He declared they were truly God's unleavened people, and instructed them to remove all the corruption and impurity in themselves.

In our spiritual pilgrimage of Holy Week, as we recall the death of Christ, there are strong ethical demands for the community of believers and for all God's people. Exhortations for moral righteousness have strong foundations in the sacrifice of the Paschal Lamb of God. The events of Maundy Thursday, of Good Friday, and of Easter are an occasion for moral renewal. It is a time for us to renew our commitment to live faithfully as God's redeemed people. When we gather at this table to remember his death, we think again of his sacrifice as the Paschal Lamb, and renew our commitment to live moral lives of faith and obedience.

Good Friday

The Tenebrae Service may be the most difficult time of the Christian Year for the preacher of the gospel. The high drama of the occasion easily tempts the preacher to overplay sentimental themes or get lost in syrupy emotions. It is, however, a time to relive the profound depth of God's mighty act to redeem and save sinful humanity. The preacher should not avoid the pain and suffering of Jesus' Passion, nor sugarcoat the pathos of his death. It is the sacred trust to retell the story with integrity, steering between tearful appeal and sensational description.

A brief meditation may be appropriate, allowing the service of darkness its full impact. The theme might invite worshipers to relive the day of crucifixion, standing together in humble remembrance at the foot of the cross. The preacher will seek to capture the calm simplicity of the African-American spiritual, "Were You There When They Crucified My Lord?" or the quiet, moving dignity of the favorite hymn, "Beneath The Cross Of Jesus."

Care must be taken in the tone and demeanor of the meditation to be sure the worship does not fall into unrelieved sorrow and grief. Even though the service recalls the death by crucifixion of the guiltless Son of God, it is an occasion for thanksgiving and joy. It was by the sacrifice of the Lamb of God our sins were forgiven and we were redeemed. The pathos of Christ's suffering should be recognized and experienced. Nevertheless, the grace of God to save a chosen people is the dominant theme of the day. Grief for the death of Jesus and joy for the mercy of God are bound in sacred worship. Sorrow for our sins is followed by thanksgiving for God's forgiveness in the full drama of the day.

Early In The Morning

Text: Mark 15:1-32

Were you there — before the first rays of dawn broke over the Holy City?

The Day of Crucifixion began very early for the High Priest, for the Jewish high court, the Sanhedrin, and for Jesus, their prisoner. It had been a long, exhaustive night. Deprived of sleep from the relentless questioning, his body aching from the blows, his face stinging from the slaps, dripping with spittle, Jesus remained in control, refusing to be intimidated by their accusations. When asked by the High Priest if he were the Messiah, the Son of the Blessed One, Jesus answered quietly, with commanding dignity, "I am." The Jewish court judged him guilty and declared him deserving of death.

Were you there — in the court of the Roman Governor?

Dawn was breaking; the first rays of the sun crept over the horizon. Pontius Pilate, the Roman governor, was summoned from his sleeping chamber to the court to hear the case of the Jews against the prophet, Jesus of Nazareth. Groggy and irritated from the early awakening, he stumbled into the court and sank heavily into the judge's chair.

It was still dark; the room was covered in shadows from the burning candles. They flickered on the bruised face of the prisoner. Still Jesus maintained the calm demeanor of a commanding presence. He would not be cowed by the trappings of power in a puppet judge who was powerless before the will of God.

Grumpily Pilate snapped, "Surely you're not the King of the Jews, are you?" Quietly Jesus answered, "That's what you say." From the multitude crowded into the courtroom, the Jews began to plead their case, accusing Jesus of blasphemy and sedition. Like a pack of snarling animals surrounding their prey, they attacked him.

Pilate asked, "Can't you see how many charges they bring against you? How do you plead? Do you have any defense?"

Jesus refused to answer.

Pilate was stupefied, realizing that Jesus was innocent of the charges. He recognized that the Jewish authorities had arrested and brought Jesus for trial for spite, jealousy, and fear for their own status. Pilate decided he would try to set Jesus free.

Were you there — among the crowd when the multitudes demanded Jesus' death?

In the jail that early morning was a notorious criminal named Barabbas. He had been arrested for murder in a rebellious fight. It was customary for the Roman governor to declare amnesty for one prisoner, and to release him during the festival. Pilate proposed to release Jesus, but the crowds, incited by the chief priests, demanded that he release Barabbas.

Still trying to set Jesus free, Pilate asked, "Then what do you want me to do with Jesus, the one you call King of the Jews?"

The crowds, who had been milling around in the courtyard since the early dawn, shouted, "Crucify him!"

Once more Pilate attempted to free Jesus, asking, "Why? What has he done?"

The crowds, agitated and victimized by the psychology of a violent mob, shouted louder and louder, "Crucify him! CRUCIFY HIM!"

Pilate, powerless in the face of mob power, gave in, and handed Jesus over to be crucified.

Were you there — in the anteroom of the military guard ordered to execute Jesus?

Perhaps you were embarrassed by the crude jokes and ribald behavior. The soldiers, restless and irritated at the early morning execution squad, first took Jesus to the barracks hall where they taunted and ridiculed him. They found a purple bathrobe, and stripping him of his own clothes, they made him put it on, as if it were the purple robe of majesty. They wove branches from thorn bushes into a crown, and crushed it down on Jesus' head. They marched around him, saluting and mocking him by shouting, "Hail, King of the Jews!"

Through all the derision and mockery, in spite of the excruciating pain, Jesus maintained his calm composure, his dignity, and control. When they grew tired of their childish play, they dressed him in his own clothes, and led him to Golgotha, to be crucified.

Were you there — along the roadside, standing beside Simon of Cyrene, when the soldiers grabbed him out of the crowd?

Perhaps you were just thankful they had skipped you and taken Simon. The day was dawning. Jesus was forced to carry his cross. Along the way, exhausted from the long tortuous night, weakened by the beatings, hungry from lack of food, Jesus stumbled and fell. The soldiers grabbed a stranger standing by the side of the road and forced him to carry the cross for Jesus. He was Simon of Cyrene, who had come to Jerusalem for the Passover. He had started home early in the morning, when he was drawn without warning into the drama of the walk to Calvary.

Were you there — when they nailed the body of Jesus to the cross?

When the death march reached the hill called Golgotha, known as the place of the Skull, the soldiers stripped Jesus naked, putting his clothes aside to gamble over later. Placing him on the cross, stretching his arms along its transcept,they pounded the crude nails through the palms of his hands and feet. They raised the cross and dropped it into the hole they had dug. They offered Jesus wine, to dull the pain, but he refused to drink. They sat down at the foot of the cross to cast lots for his clothes and to wait for him to die.

It was just nine o' clock in the morning, the third hour of the day. What if we had been there that early morning almost 2,000 years ago. How would we have reacted to the events that led to Jesus' crucifixion?

Perhaps we would have tried to persuade the authorities Jesus really was the Son of God. We might have supported him in his preaching a new covenant of God's love. But our record of accepting religious doctrines that are new or different has not been good. Our tolerance of ideas and spiritual practices that are unfamiliar or seem different from our own faith is short indeed. We protect the status quo; we support the religious institutions, and are hesitant to consider someone else's expression of faith. We are quick to brand as heretics anyone who disagrees with us, and are slow to consider that perhaps we can learn something new about what God is doing in the world. Yet we will insist that this was Jesus. Surely we would have believed him.

Perhaps we would have protested against the injustice of their mocking trials, against the scheming, conniving political conspiracy, against the false testimony to convict an innocent person. But our record of protest against political injustice has not been good. We have often been hesitant to stand up against powerful authority, even when we have felt it was evil. We stand idly by when political prisoners have been incarcerated in cruel, miserable jail cells, when they were tortured and beaten and killed. When American hostages were imprisoned we rose up in patriotic fury, but where were we when Nelson Mandela was jailed? Or Bishop Mendoza was killed? When hate crimes against homosexuals killed a young college student and a cruel dragging death left an African-American dead? Yet we will insist this was Jesus. Surely we would have tried to set him free.

Perhaps we would have tried to shield Jesus from the blows, to refute the lying witnesses, to wipe the spittle from his face. We might have tried to protect him. But our record of involvement in unpopular causes has not been good. To be sure, we have never hidden behind locked windows, refusing even to call the cops, while thugs killed innocent victims in the street. But we have steadfastly minded our own business when issues such as capital punishment, partial birth abortions, euthanasia, gun control, or campaign funding reform were being debated. It is so much easier not to get involved; so much less threatening not to take a stand. Let the fanatics pursue their causes. We will devote our energies to more spiritual matters. We will insist this was Jesus. Surely we would have taken a stand for him.

What if we had been present that early morning so long ago?

Tonight we are present, at the foot of the cross. We have come, confessing our sins, acknowledging our self-centered pride, our intolerance, our self-righteous faith, admitting our fear of powerful authorities and our failure to condemn injustice, confessing our weakness in standing for what we know is right. And tonight we hear from the crucified Lord, who died to save us, words of forgiveness, spoken in the quiet, calm authority of merciful grace. Tonight we know our sins are forgiven, and we are redeemed. Tonight we believe that by the death of Jesus Christ, we are saved.

www.ingramcontent.com/pod-product-compliance
Lightning Source LLC
Chambersburg PA
CBHW071800040426
42446CB00012B/2643

Filling the Hungry with Good Things

*Cycle C Sermons for
Proper 13 Through Proper 22
Based on the Gospel Texts*

Richard A. Jensen

CSS Publishing Company, Inc.
Lima, Ohio

FILLING THE HUNGRY WITH GOOD THINGS

FIRST EDITION
Copyright © 2012
by CSS Publishing Co., Inc.

Published by CSS Publishing Company, Inc., Lima, Ohio 45807. All rights reserved. No part of this publication may be reproduced in any manner whatsoever without the prior permission of the publisher, except in the case of brief quotations embodied in critical articles and reviews. Inquiries should be addressed to: CSS Publishing Company, Inc., Permissions Department, 5450 N. Dixie Highway, Lima, Ohio 45807.

Scripture quotations are from the New Revised Standard Version of the Bible. Copyright 1989 by the Division of Christian Education of the National Council of the Churches of Christ in the USA. Used by permission.

Library of Congress Cataloging-in-Publication Data
Jensen, Richard A.
   Filling the hungry with good things : cycle C sermons for Pentecost 2, Proper 13 through Proper 22, based on the Gospel texts / Richard A. Jensen. -- 1st ed.
     p. cm.
   ISBN 0-7880-2680-1 (alk. paper)
   1. Bible. N.T. Luke--Sermons. 2. Pentecost season--Sermons. 3. Common lectionary (1992) I. Title.

BS2595.54.J46 2012
252'.64--dc23

2012004189

For more information about CSS Publishing Company resources, visit our website at www.csspub.com, email us at csr@csspub.com, or call (800) 241-4056.

ISBN-13: 978-0-7880-2680-5
ISBN-10: 0-7880-2680-1
                                      PRINTED IN USA